LEVEL 5

Written by: Andy Hopkins and Jocelyn Potter
Series Editor: Melanie Williams

Pearson Education Limited
Edinburgh Gate, Harlow,
Essex CM20 2JE, England
and Associated Companies throughout the world.

ISBN: 978-1-4082-8698-2

This edition first published by Pearson Education Ltd 2014
3 5 7 9 10 8 6 4 2
Text copyright © Pearson Education Ltd 2014

The moral rights of the author have been asserted
in accordance with the Copyright Designs and Patents Act 1988

Set in 15/19pt OT Fiendstar
Printed in China
SWTC/02

Acknowledgements
The publisher would like to thank the following for their kind permission to reproduce their photographs:
(Key: b-bottom; c-centre; l-left; r-right; t-top)

Corbis: Richard H. Cohen 26; **Getty Images:** H. Armstrong Roberts 21, Lewis W. Hine / Archive Photos 12;
Mary Evans Picture Library: Everett Collection 18, © Illustrated London News Ltd 10; **SuperStock:**
Anthony Butera 23, Kablonk 29; **TopFoto:** The Granger Collection 5, 14

All other images © Pearson Education

Every effort has been made to trace the copyright holders and we apologise in advance
for any unintentional omissions. We would be pleased to insert the appropriate
acknowledgement in any subsequent edition of this publication.

Illustrations: Lizzy Stewart

Published by Pearson Education Ltd

For a complete list of the titles available in the Pearson English Kids Readers series, please go to
www.pearsonenglishkidsreaders.com. Alternatively, write to your local Pearson Education office or to
Pearson English Readers Marketing Department, Pearson Education, Edinburgh Gate, Harlow, Essex CM202JE, England.

CHAPTER 1

The Open Door

'The Statue of Liberty!' Patrick shouted.
'We're here, Ronan! The United States of America!'

Ronan ran to the side of the ship.

'It's huge!' he said. 'And look at those mountains behind it!'

His brother laughed. 'They're not mountains. They're skyscrapers — the tallest buildings in the world. That's the city of New York. But first, we go there.' Patrick pointed to a small island. 'All new immigrants have to go to Ellis Island.'

'Stay in line!' shouted a man in uniform.

The brothers were on their way into Ellis Island's Great Hall. They went up the stairs with hundreds of others.

Doctors watched from the top. One put a mark on a young woman's back.

'Hold your head up, Ronan,' said Patrick quietly. 'They're looking for people who are ill. They don't want sick people in this country.'

'What will happen to her?' Ronan asked.

'I don't know. Perhaps they'll send her home.'

Ellis Island

Between 1892 and 1924, 12 million immigrants arrived at Ellis Island. In one year, 1907, more than a million came. The immigration station grew larger, with more beds, kitchens and hospitals. Most people only spent a few hours on the island and then entered the country. Some sick people had to spend weeks there. Other people had to stay there before officials sent them home. The United States did not want them.

Today, Ellis Island is a museum.

The man at the desk looked at the papers in front of him. 'You're from Ireland?'

'Yes,' Patrick answered. 'And this is my brother.'

'Can you read and write?' the official asked Ronan.

'No, sir,' Ronan answered. 'But I can learn – and I can work.'

The official looked at Patrick. 'So your uncle paid for your tickets. Did he send you any money?'

'Yes, sir.' Patrick carefully pulled $50 from his pocket.

The official's face was not friendly. His questions came fast.

'Will he let us in?' Ronan thought. He could see the fear in his brother's eyes.

Then the man smiled and gave Patrick two cards. 'You can go downstairs to the boat,' he said.

The boys ran down the stairs to start their new lives. It was 1921, and now they had a future. Now they had hope.

CHAPTER 2

Leaving Home

Six months earlier, Patrick and Ronan were at home in Ireland.

'Listen, boys,' their father said. 'This is a letter from your Uncle Dermot in New York. Inside are two boat tickets – one for you, Patrick and one for you, Ronan.'

Patrick's mouth fell open. 'But Father, Colleen … '

'Colleen can wait,' said his father. 'There's nothing for you here. Your future's in America. There's work there. You can send some money home for your family.'

Ronan was excited. New York! His father was a poor farmer. The land was not his, and he made little money. Surely life was better in America?

'When did Uncle Dermot leave Ireland?' he asked.

'Twenty years ago,' Father said. 'He's doing well. My grandfather went too, you know. He left in the 1840s, but the family stayed here. There was no money for tickets.'

'Was life difficult then?' Patrick asked.

'Terrible. It was the time of the Potato Famine.'

The Irish Potato Famine

In 1845, disease ruined the potato crop, the most important food for poor Irish people. In the next six years, there were few potatoes. More than a million people died. Another million left Ireland at that time. Many went to England, but half travelled to North America. Most Irish immigrants to the United States had little money, so they stayed near New York. By 1855, 25 per cent of the people in the city were Irish.

It was a beautiful spring morning. Patrick and Colleen sat beside the river.

'Colleen, I love you so much,' he said.

'And I love you too, Patrick Dooley,' she answered.

He smiled – a sad smile. 'I'm going to America with young Ronan to find work.'

She said nothing, but a tear fell from her eye.

'Will you wait for me, Colleen? I'll send a ticket for you when I have money. '

'Oh yes, Patrick, I'll wait.'

After World War I

Irish men and women were not the only Europeans who had to emigrate in the 1920s. In World War I (1914-18), people lost family, friends, homes and land. They were hungry and they had no work. The map of Europe changed. After the war, more than 15 million people wanted to travel to North America. But there was not enough work for Americans, so from 1921 the United States only took about 350,000 new immigrants each year.

CHAPTER 3

Journey to Another Land

'This is home for the next six days, Ronan,' said Patrick.

The boys were on the ship now. There were people everywhere.

Ronan looked around him with wide eyes. 'It's very big.'

'The *Baltic* carries about 3,000 people,' Patrick laughed.

'3,000? Where will we all sleep?'

'Don't worry. You'll have a bed. And there are bathrooms and sitting-rooms – and food too. It was very different when Father's grandfather travelled to America.'

In the 1840s

At the time of the Irish Potato Famine, the journey to New York was terrible. Ships brought cargo to Ireland and returned to North America with passengers. Rooms were dirty, with little air or light. People with money brought food with them. The poorest stayed hungry, and there was never enough clean water. One in seven passengers died on the long journey. Over the years, more than 50,000 Irish people died on these 'coffin ships'.

The ship left Queenstown, in the south of Ireland.

'I'm going to look around,' said Ronan later.

'OK,' Patrick said. 'Take your bag. There are thieves everywhere.'

Ronan went outside. He opened a door and went up a lot of stairs to the top part of the ship. Through a window, he could see a huge, beautiful room full of rich people. He put his bag down.

'Hey, you!' a man shouted.

Ronan turned and ran back down the stairs.

'Where's your bag?' Patrick shouted.

'Oh, no!' Ronan cried. His clothes were in it – and family photos.

'Is this yours?' asked a voice. A girl of about twelve in a beautiful, expensive dress stood in the doorway. 'I'm Anna. I saw you upstairs.'

She gave Ronan his bag.

'Thank you!' Ronan said. 'I'm Ronan. This is Patrick. We're going to our uncle in New York.'

'I'm with my parents,' Anna said. 'I can't stay now, but perhaps we'll meet again.'

CHAPTER 4

A New Life

'Don't be afraid, Ronan!' Uncle Dermot smiled.

They were on a train high above the street, but many buildings were taller. There were cars and people everywhere.

'New Yorkers are always busy!' shouted Dermot over the noise of the train and the cars.

The buildings outside were older now. The people in the street looked poorer.

Dermot stood up. 'Here we are,' he said. 'Hell's Kitchen is full of Irish people. You'll feel at home.'

Immigrant Homes

When immigrants arrived in New York, they often wanted to be with people from their country. They wanted to speak their own language and eat food from home. Many Irish people went to Hell's Kitchen in Manhattan. The city centre also had a Chinatown and a Koreatown. At one time, 40,000 Italians lived in New York's Little Italy. People from other countries had places in many parts of the city. New York was full of immigrants.

'My friend Liam is a builder,' Dermot told Patrick. 'He's working on a new skyscraper. You can work with him.'

Patrick looked worried. 'I want to work, but I'm a farmer. I don't know anything about building,' he said.

'Just listen to Liam and work hard,' Dermot said. 'You'll be fine. Some of the other men were Irish farmers too.'

'Is the work dangerous, Uncle?' Ronan asked.

'It can be,' Dermot answered. 'Patrick will have to be careful.'

'Can I work on the skyscraper too?' asked Ronan.

'No. Here, young man, children have to go to school until the age of fourteen,' Aunt Nora said.

'But I don't want to go to school,' said Ronan.

'Listen to me,' said his aunt. 'This is your opportunity. Learn to read and write. Learn your numbers. Learn about America. In this wonderful country, you can have a better life. But first you must study. Then, perhaps, you'll have a great future.'

The American Dream

Many Americans believed in 'The American Dream', and new immigrants believed in it too. They were usually poor when they arrived in the United States. But if they worked hard, change was possible. There were, they believed, ways up from the bottom to the top of the ladder – to a good job, a nice home and money. Your birthplace, your parents and your past did not matter. If you wanted a great future, you could get it.

CHAPTER 5

The Children's Story

Ronan's first day at school felt strange. Many of the children in his class were younger than him. He wanted to learn, but it was hard work. At last the day ended.

'Ronan, is that you?'

He turned and saw Anna, the English girl from the ship! They talked happily.

'Is reading difficult for you too?' he asked her.

'No, Ronan. I can read well. I'll help you,' she answered.

From that day, they were friends.

Immigrants at School

In New York, at that time, children had to go to school until fourteen years old. Three-quarters of the children had one or two parents who were born in another country. Many immigrant children lived unhealthy lives in poor flats with little clean air. They needed book education and health education. They also needed to learn about the American way of life. Schools had to be parents, doctors and social workers. Slowly, young immigrants became Americans.

'I saw you with a girl yesterday, Ronan. Who was she?' asked Aunt Nora.

'She's an English girl. I met her on the ship,' answered Ronan.

'English!' his aunt cried. 'Stay away from her, my boy. The English are no good!'

The next day, Ronan told Anna about his aunt's words.

'My father says the same about Irish boys,' she answered sadly.

'But we can be friends, Anna. We're in a new country now. We're Americans!' said Ronan.

'Ronan Dooley?' the teacher said loudly from the classroom door. 'Come with me.'

Ronan followed her to an office. Inside was his uncle.

'Sit down, Ronan. I have to tell you something,' Dermot said.

'Is it about Anna? She's my friend and I want to see her ...'

'Stop, Ronan. It's not about Anna,' said Dermot. 'It's about Patrick ...'

Ronan looked at him. He knew.

'I'm sorry, Ronan. There was a terrible accident this morning ...'

CHAPTER 6

Immigrants Today

Today New York, the largest city in the United States, is still a place of hope for new immigrants. One in three people was born in another country, and you can hear hundreds of languages on the streets. In about half of all homes, English is not the first language. Shops and restaurants sell food from every part of the world, and people from some countries bring their celebrations into the streets.

'Ronan Dooley was my mother's grandfather. He came to this country at your age with nothing — no money and no education. After his brother, Patrick, died, he had to send money back to his family in Ireland. He worked after school, and he studied hard. After college, he became a lawyer, and then a politician. He helped poor people and immigrants because he understood them. He wanted to make the United States a better country.'

'What happened to Patrick's girlfriend, Colleen?' the boy asked.

'She never left Ireland, and she never married. But Ronan married Anna, and they had six children. When Ronan came to New York nearly a hundred years ago, most immigrants married people from their own country. But Ronan and Anna didn't mind about the political problems between England and Ireland. They were in the United States, a land of immigrants. Our differences are interesting – but we are all Americans.'

People on the Move

Every year, about 3 per cent of the world's population moves to another country. Millions of people leave their homes from fear of war, politics or famine in their own country. Some return when life is better. Many poor people leave home because they want to work. They often send money back to their families, and this helps poorer countries. Most emigrants are looking for better opportunities. They are looking for a land of new hope.

Glossary

disease (n) p10   If you have a disease, you are ill. People, animals and plants can get diseases.

education (n) p23   You get an education at school and at college.

emigrate (v) p12   If you emigrate, you leave your country and live in another country. Many **emigrants** never return to their own countries.

enter (v) p5   When you enter a place, you go into it.

famine (n) p9   When there is a famine, a lot of people have little or no food for a long time.

fear (n) p7   When something frightens you, you feel fear.

health (n) p23   If you have good health, you are not ill. A **healthy** person is strong and usually in good health. An **unhealthy** person is ill, or often ill.

immigrant (n) p3   An immigrant comes to live in a country from another country. There was a lot of Irish **immigration** to the United States.

official (n) p5   Officials work for a city or a country, so other people have to listen to them.

opportunity (n) p20   An opportunity makes something possible.

passenger (n) p14   A passenger is a traveller on a bus, a train or a ship.

politician (n) p27   Good politicians work for the people who choose them. In their **political** lives, they try to make a town or a country better. **Politics** is a politician's work and ideas.

population (n) p29   The population of a place is all the people in it.

war (n) p12   In a war, countries fight.

worry (v) p13   If a problem worries you, it makes you unhappy. If you think about a problem a lot, you are **worried**.

Before You Read

❶ **Look at the picture on page 3 and answer these questions.**

   a Is this a story about the present, future or past?

   b Where are the boys in the picture?

   c Where are they going to?

   d How do they feel?

   e Why do you think they feel this way?

   f Why do you think the book is called *A Land of New Hope*?

❷ **Look quickly through the book. Match the names with these people.**

   1 Ronan

   2 Patrick

   3 Colleen

   4 Anna

   5 Uncle Dermot

(a)

(b)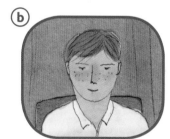

(c)

(d)

(e)

Activity page ②

After You Read

1 **Finish the sentences.**

a Patrick and Ronan went to New York for

   1 a better life.   **2** love.   **3** a holiday.

b They arrived in America in

   1 1952.   **2** 2012.   **3** 1921.

c More than a million people left Ireland between 1845 and 1851 because of

   1 the bad weather. **2** World War I.   **3** the Potato Famine.

d Uncle Dermot lived in

   1 Little Italy.   **2** Hell's Kitchen.   **3** Chinatown.

e Ronan married

   1 Anna.   **2** Nora.   **3** Colleen.

2 **Answer the questions.**

a What job did Patrick get in New York?

b What happened to Patrick?

c Did Ronan work at first?

d Why did Ronan's aunt tell him to stay away from Anna?

e What happened to Ronan when he was older?

3 **What do you think?**

a Why do families leave their country and become immigrants?

b How do they feel when they leave home? Why?

c How do they feel when they arrive in a new country? Why?